A GLOBAL FUND FOR
Children
BOOK

Music Everywhere!

A young violinist
practices in her
home. VENEZUELA

MAYA AJMERA

ELISE HOFER DERSTINE

CYNTHIA PON

Charlesbridge

We love music!

Singing in a children's chorus. SPAIN

A Hmong boy plays the qeej (pronounced *gheng*). LAOS

Playing the clarinet in a children's musical. UNITED KINGDOM

Dancing to drumbeats. GHANA

Blowing on a conch shell at the Festival of Pacific Arts. COOK ISLANDS

Kids everywhere make music every day.

Step dancing at a traditional Irish
music festival. UNITED KINGDOM

Clapping with joy. INDIA

A boy with bells on his boots dances in a parade. ARGENTINA

We clap our hands and stomp our feet . . .

. . . singing and humming our favorite tunes.

Chanting in a Coptic choir. EGYPT

A Wixárika boy performs a song that
proudly proclaims his heritage. MEXICO

Schoolchildren sing a song
they wrote together. JAPAN

We play musical instruments of all shapes and sizes.

Buddhist novices play dungchen (long horns) in a temple. BHUTAN

Orchestra members play the yueqin (moon lute). CHINA

A junior bagpiper at a Highland Games in Scotland. UNITED KINGDOM

We blow and whistle,

A Jewish boy blows a shofar
made of a ram's horn. ISRAEL

Playing a traditional Andean zampoña. PERU

Surrounded by modern and traditional instruments in a music shop. MOROCCO

A young girl in traditional dress plucks the strings of a fiddle. POLAND

pluck and strum,

scrape, rattle, and shake!

Jamming with drum and maracas. BELGIUM

Beating a taiko drum at a
Shinto celebration. JAPAN

Tapping out a light-hearted rhythm. MALAWI

We bang and *thump thump thump!*

It's fun to practice and perform.

Practicing pitches in singing class. RUSSIA

Playing the reyong in a
gamelan orchestra.
INDONESIA

Learning to play the steel drum at
a neighborhood arts center. USA

Music has many moods.

Young musicians deep into a violin lesson. VENEZUELA

Strumming her favorite instrument. GABON

Singing in a children's gospel choir. USA

Music is everywhere—
at home, at school . . .

Improvising with hands and chairs. TOGO

Banging on pots in
the kitchen. USA

Finding refuge in a song. IRAQ

. . . in our neighborhoods,

Playing a tambourine in the park. ARGENTINA

Boys show off instruments they made at a bluegrass festival. FRANCE

Friends enjoying ukulele music. USA

and even at the beach.

Music brings people together—

Music lessons at a camp for Palestinian refugees.
WEST BANK/PALESTINIAN TERRITORIES

A brother and sister play
a duet. NEW ZEALAND

Performing at a school for children with special abilities. TAIWAN

jumping, swaying, and dancing to the beat.

We love music!

A young tambourinaire leaps, drumsticks in hand. BURUNDI

Drumming at a Carnival celebration. BRAZIL

Playing guitar at preschool. USA

Kids make music all over the world.

Strumming a mandolin at Ba Futuru, an organization that uses music, drama, and dance to help communities heal from trauma. TIMOR-LESTE

Canada

USA

Mexico

Cook Islands

Venezuela

Peru

Brazil

Argentina

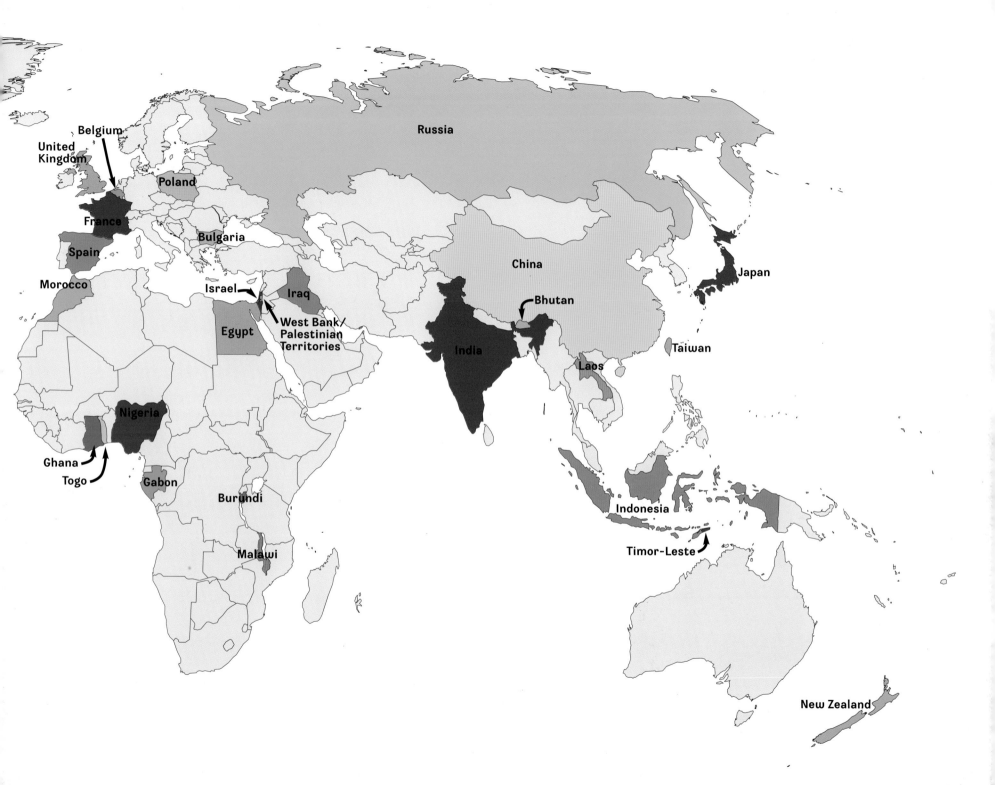

Belgium

United
Kingdom

Poland

Russia

France

Spain

Bulgaria

China

Japan

Morocco

Israel

Iraq

Bhutan

Egypt

West Bank/
Palestinian
Territories

Taiwan

India

Laos

Nigeria

Ghana

Togo

Gabon

Burundi

Indonesia

Malawi

Timor-Leste

New Zealand

Make Your Own Instruments

Many musical instruments can be made from everyday materials.

BEAN TAMBOURINE: Color or decorate the bottom of two paper plates. Ask an adult to help you staple the plates together around the edge, leaving an opening at the top. Drop some dried beans into the opening and staple the instrument shut. Now shake out a rhythm with your new tambourine!

HOMEMADE RATTLES: You can make rattles out of all kinds of materials. Try filling an empty spice container with pennies, beads, or uncooked rice. Cardboard tubes, aluminum cans, and plastic bottles also make good instruments. Containers of different shapes, sizes, and materials will make different sounds. Experiment with fillings, too, so no two rattles sound the same.

GLASS HARP: Ask an adult to help you fill some sturdy glasses or jars with different amounts of water. Gently tap the side of each glass with a spoon. Can you order the glasses from lowest pitch to highest?

Join a School Music Group

School is a great place to explore music. You might enjoy playing an instrument in the school band or orchestra, or singing songs in the choir. Does your school put on plays or musicals?

Sisters play a glass harp in their backyard. UNITED KINGDOM

Dance to the Beat!

We can listen to music with our whole bodies, not just our ears! Try making up a dance to music, matching your movements to the mood. Is the music slow, heavy, and gloomy? Or fast and cheerful? Does the mood stay the same for the whole song? Try choosing two very different songs and see how your dances change.

Find Music in Your Community

You can find music almost anywhere. Summer concerts in the park, parades, and street performances are just a few ways to listen to music in your neighborhood. Music flows through markets, places of worship, and art centers. Where do you hear music in your neighborhood?

Performing a traditional festival dance. NIGERIA

Try Out New Tunes

Most public libraries have music you can take home, just like checking out a book. You can listen to steel drums from Trinidad, or flamenco guitars from Spain. Hear dramatic tango music played by an Argentinean orchestra, or romping fiddle tunes performed by an American bluegrass band. Try checking out music you've never heard of before—you never know what new sounds you'll discover!

Words to Know

ANDEAN MUSIC: music of various styles rooted in the traditional cultures of the Northern and Central Andes mountains in South America. The Andean peoples are the indigenous (original) inhabitants of the area.

ANISHINAABE: one of the largest indigenous tribes living in North America today, also known as Chippewa or Ojibwa. The name Anishinaabe means "original people" in their language.

BLUEGRASS: a genre of music that developed in the Appalachian region of the United States. Bluegrass has roots in African American, Scottish, Irish, English, and other musical traditions.

BUDDHISM: a faith whose followers seek to end suffering by living according to the teachings of the Buddha (meaning "one who is awake").

CARNIVAL: a grand festival held before Lent, a season of the Christian calendar. Popular around the world, Carnival combines parades, masquerades, music, food, and dancing.

COPTIC MUSIC: music of the Coptic Orthodox Church, a Christian church founded in Egypt. Coptic choirs sing or chant melodies a cappella (without accompanying instruments) except for small percussion instruments, such as the triangle or hand cymbals.

DUNGCHEN: long horns, usually played in multiples, that are widely used in Tibetan Buddhist culture. They are said to sound like the trumpeting of elephants.

GAMELAN: a traditional Indonesian music ensemble that often accompanies rituals, dances, or puppet theater.

GOSPEL MUSIC: a genre of American folk music characterized by strong vocals and lyrics rooted in Christian spirituality. Gospel has origins in Europe, Africa, and the African American slave experience.

HMONG PEOPLE: an ethnic minority group native to the mountainous region of several Asian countries, including China, Vietnam, Laos, and Thailand.

MANDOLIN: a musical instrument in the lute family, played by plucking or strumming.

MARACA: Latin American percussion instrument traditionally made of a gourd shell filled with dried beans. Maracas are usually played in pairs.

QEEJ (pronounced *gheng*): an instrument made of bamboo pipes of varying lengths, curved in an arc and rooted in a wooden wind chamber. During New Year festivals young Hmong men demonstrate their musical and athletic prowess by playing the qeej while performing somersaults and dance-like movements.

REYONG: an Indonesian (Balinese) instrument consisting of several metal gongs suspended side by side on a frame.

An Anishinaabe girl plays a drum made of birch bark and rawhide. CANADA

SHINTOISM: a faith practiced in Japan whose followers worship many gods and spirits.

SHOFAR: a trumpet made from a ram's horn. It is used on occasions sacred to the Jewish religion.

TAIKO: literally, "great drum." Taiko refers to a variety of Japanese drums that trace back to mythical, ceremonial, martial, and court origins.

TAMBOURINAIRES: traditional Burundian drummers famous for their acrobatic displays.

UKULELE: a small four-stringed guitar. The ukulele is a Hawaiian instrument with Portuguese roots. Its name means "jumping flea."

WIXÁRIKA: an indigenous ethnic group native to parts of western central Mexico. Though commonly known as

Huichol, they refer to themselves as Wixaritari ("the people") in their native language.

YUEQIN: a traditional Chinese stringed instrument, also called a "moon-lute" for its round shape.

ZAMPOÑA: a Peruvian panpipe. Zampoñas are traditionally made from reeds harvested from the banks of Lake Titicaca high in the mountains.

For all children who delight in music—may it bring them joy throughout their lives.—M. A.

For my sister, Alexandra, who filled our childhood home with her beautiful voice and skilled piano playing, and lots of New Kids on the Block. Thanks for making the music for my memories.—E. H. D.

For my sister, Linda, who loves, and plays, music animato, appassionato, and grazioso.—C. P.

The co-authors of *Music Everywhere!* wish to thank Olivia Cadaval (Smithsonian Center for Folklife and Cultural Heritage), Judith Gray (American Folklife Center, Library of Congress), and D. A. Sonneborn (Smithsonian Folkways Recordings) for their generous review of the captions and glossary during the book's development process. Sincere thanks also to Victoria Dunning, VP of Programs at The Global Fund for Children, and our friends at Charlesbridge Publishing for harmony and collaboration.

Music Everywhere! was developed by The Global Fund for Children (www.globalfundforchildren.org), a nonprofit organization committed to advancing the dignity of children and youth around the world. Global Fund for Children books teach young people to value diversity and help them become productive and caring citizens of the world.

Developed by The Global Fund for Children
1101 Fourteenth Street, NW, Suite 420
Washington, DC 20005
(202) 331-9003 • www.globalfundforchildren.org

Published by Charlesbridge
85 Main Street
Watertown, MA 02472
(617) 926-0329 • www.charlesbridge.com

Part of the proceeds from this book's sales will be donated to The Global Fund for Children to support innovative community-based organizations that serve the world's most vulnerable children and youth. Details about the donation of royalties can be obtained by writing to Charlesbridge Publishing and The Global Fund for Children.

Library of Congress Cataloging-in-Publication Data
Ajmera, Maya.
Music everywhere! / Maya Ajmera, Elise Hofer Derstine, and Cynthia Pon.
    pages cm
"A Global Fund for Children book."
    ISBN 978-1-57091-936-7 (reinforced for library use)
    ISBN 978-1-57091-937-4 (softcover)
    ISBN 978-1-60734-670-8 (ebook)
1. Music appreciation—Juvenile literature. I. Derstine, Elise Hofer. II. Pon, Cynthia. III. Title.
ML3928.A36 2013
781.1'7—dc23   2012027113

Printed in China
(hc) 10 9 8 7 6 5 4 3 2
(sc) 10 9 8 7 6 5 4 3 2

Display type set in Spumoni, text type set in Adobe Garamond Pro
Color separations by KHL Chroma Graphics, Singapore
Printed by Imago in China
Production supervision by Brian G. Walker
Designed by Susan Mallory Sherman

Photo Credits

FRONT COVER: © Tibor Bognar / Art Directors.
BACK COVER: © Charlotte Oestervang.
TITLE PAGE: p. 1: © Carlos Cazalis / Corbis.
WE LOVE MUSIC!: p. 2: left, © Sheila Burnett / ArenaPal / The Image Works; top right, © Tolo Balaguer / Agefotostock.com; bottom right, © Victoria Vorreiter / www.TribalMusicAsia.com. p. 3: left, © Alida Latham / DanitaDelimont.com; right, © Anders Ryman / Alamy.
CLAP AND STOMP: p. 4: © Klaus Werner-Friedric / Agefotostock.com. p. 5: left, © Francois Werli / Alamy; right, © Wendy Kaveney / Jaynes Gallery / DanitaDelimont.com.
SING AND HUM: p. 6: left, © Alfredo Estrella / AFP / Getty Images; right, © Sean Sprague / The Image Works. p. 7: © Art in All of Us / Stephanie Rabemiafara.
SHAPES AND SIZES: p. 8: left, © Art Wolfe / www.artwolfe.com; center, © George Holton / Photo Researchers, Inc. p. 9: © Jon Arnold Images / DanitaDelimont.com.
BLOW AND PLUCK: p. 10: left, © Travel Pix / Taxi / Getty Images; right, © Oliver Weiken / EPA / Landov. p. 11: left, © Pete Oxford / DanitaDelimont.com; right, © Bert Wiklund.
SCRAPE AND BANG: p. 12: left, © A. Chederros / Onoky / Aurora Photos; center, © Photo Japan / Agefotostock.com. p. 13: © REUTERS / Mike Hutchings / Landov.
PRACTICE AND PERFORM: p. 14: © Ken Scicluna / awl-images.com. p. 15: left, © Blaine Harrington; right, © Ellen B. Senisi / The Image Works.
MOODS: p. 16: left, © REUTERS / Jorge Silva / Landov; right, © Spectrum Photofile. p. 17: © N. Joel Ward, courtesy of Washington Performing Arts Society's Children of the Gospel Choir.
HOME AND SCHOOL: p. 18: left, © Alida Latham / DanitaDelimont.com; right, © Michael Newman / Photoedit.com. p. 19: © REUTERS / Julie Adnan / Landov.
NEIGHBORHOODS AND BEACH: p. 20: left, © Terry Vine / Stone / Getty Images; center, © Kayte Deioma. p. 21: © Photo Resource Hawaii / DanitaDelimont.com.
BRINGING PEOPLE TOGETHER: p. 22: left, © Rina Castelnuovo / The *New York Times* / Redux; right, © Donald Iain Smith / Flickr / Getty Images. p. 23: © Sean Sprague / StillPictures / Aurora Photos.
WE LOVE MUSIC!: p. 24: left, © Tom Martin / awl-images.com; center, © Ingrid Firmhofer / LOOK / Getty Images. p. 25: © Ellen B. Senisi / The Image Works / The Image Works.
BACK MATTER: p. 26: © Ba Futuru. p. 28: © Helene Rogers / Art Directors. p. 29: © Patrick Olear / Photoedit.com. p. 31: © NativeStock.com / Marilyn Angel Wynn.